LUDLOW FAIR
and
HOME FREE!

BY
LANFORD WILSON

★

★

DRAMATISTS
PLAY SERVICE
INC.

LUDLOW FAIR

A Play in One Act

LUDLOW FAIR was first produced by Joe Cino at the Caffe Cino, in New York City, on February 1, 1965. It was directed by, and the set design was by, Neil Flanagan; the lighting design was by Dennis Parichy; and the stage manager was Renée Mauguin. The cast was as follows:

RACHEL .... Martha Galphin
AGNES .... Jennie Ventriss

CHARACTERS

RACHEL, an attractive young woman in her mid-twenties.
AGNES, on the heavy side, busty, not unattractive, but no raving
    beauty, in her mid-twenties. She would be considered "a
    great deal of fun."

LUDLOW FAIR

The bedroom of their apartment. Two twin beds on one wall, a vanity dresser across the room. A desk with books. The room is neat and in good taste. On the table between the beds is a phone. On the desk, is a dictionary, among other books; on the vanity is, among the usual paraphernalia, a box of large hair rollers and a bottle of nail polish. One exit is to the bathroom, another to the living room. Rachel wears a nightgown and robe; Agnes, pajamas and robe.

RACHEL.   *(Wandering around the room alone. She is restless; she looks at one thing and another. Finally, quite to herself.)* Oh, God; I think you're losing your head. I think you're going stark raving insane and you've got no one in this ever-loving world, sweetheart, to blame except yourself. And maybe Joe. But then.... Are you losing it? Hmm? Let's see. *(She pinches herself firmly. For a full two seconds she considers the effect. Matter-of-factly.)* Ouch! *(Yelling toward the bathroom.)* Agnes? *(Waits.)* How long are you going to take, anyway?
AGNES.   *(Offstage, from the bathroom.)* What?
RACHEL.   I said, are you about through in there?
AGNES.   In a minute.
RACHEL.   You said that an hour ago. *(She waits for an answer, none comes. Rubbing her arm.)* What a stupid thing to do. That's no kind of test of insanity, anyway. That's for drunkenness or sleep-walking or disorderly conduct or something. How do you know if your faculties are ebbing away from you, anyway? *(Seriously considering.)* You go to an analyst, what does he do? You lie down on the couch, what does he do? Ha! No, a respectable analyst, what does he do? You lie — A quick little word association. You can't give yourself a word — well, why not? *(Sits quickly on the chair at the desk.)* Ready? Ready. Very well, when I say a word you come in with the very first word that pops into your head. Yes, I understand. Very

7

well. *(Pause, tries for a split second to think of a word. Finally.)* Word. *(Immediately answers.)* Word! *(Blank pause.)* Dog. *(Absolutely blank for the count of six. Aside.)* Oh, for Christ's sake.... *(Intense concentration. Mumbles.)* Dog. *(Breaking away, then firmly.)* Jesus Chri — DOG! *(Pause. With the same studied intensity.)* CAT! *(Aside.)* For Christ's sake — well, that's it — cat. Keep it up. Cat. *(Same amount of pause between words, same intensity to each word.)* Rat. Mouse. House. Rat. Dog. Cat. Mouse. Louse. Bat. Pat. Fat. Louse. *(Breaking away.)* Fat louse, Jesus Christ. Rat, cat, mouse, louse, bat, house; you don't need an analyst you need an exterminator. You can't associate with yourself. Even words. *(Calling to no one.)* Joe! *(Sees the dictionary on the desk, puts it in her lap.)* Well, why not? As long as you don't know the word that's coming up. Now the first word that pops into your head. *(Answering herself.)* Yes, I understand. *(She opens the book, looks down, closes it. Flatly.)* Knickerbocker! *(Sighs slowly, then with redetermination.)* All right, I'll play your stupid game with you. Holiday. Take that. *(Opens the book again. Looks more closely. Reading.)* Phen-a-kis-to-scope. *(Pause. Looking at it. Continues reading.)* "An instrument resembling the zoe-thrope in principle and use. One form consists of a disk with the figures arranged about the center, with radial slits" — *(Aside.)* Radial slits? *(Continues to read.)* "Radial slits through which the figures are viewed — *(Becoming amused.)* — by means of a mirror." *(Closing the dictionary.)* But what's it for? Phen-a-kis-to-scope. Very well. *(She gets up, wanders to the dresser. As though she were thinking.)* Phenakistoscope. Ah, ah ... Zoethrope! Naturally. *(Sitting at the dresser, the dictionary open in front of her, she quite casually opens the nail polish and pours an amount on one page, shuts the dictionary firmly, props it open again, like an easel against the back of the vanity. Studies it carefully from some distance.)* Ah.... Oh, ah.... A tree. *(Aside.)* A tree. That couldn't possibly mean anything. *(Looks back at it, studying.)* Ah. Ah. Your trouble is you have no imagination, Rachel. You're not nuts, you're just dull. Okay.... Ah. An ostrich. That's a little better. An ostrich. Eating. *(Considering her progress.)* An ostrich, huh? That's vaguely phallic, you know. Well, vaguely. *(Shutting the book.)* That's the trouble with those things, when they start working you're in trouble. *(She gets up, carrying the book, rubs her arm.)* If you don't learn to stop pinching yourself. *(Calling.)* Agnes? Are you ever

8

getting out of there?

AGNES. *(Offstage.)* What? I'll be out in a minute. Christ.

RACHEL. You said that an hour ago. *(She lays the book back on the dresser, wanders about.)* There's nothing wrong with you, Rachel, except you're given to talking to yourself — *driven* to talking to yourself. *(Falls down on her bed, stretched out, looking up blankly.)* Long pointless conversations before retiring. Well, doctor — it's this way. Joe turned out to be a rat. But then I think I knew that before he turned out. *(Props herself on one elbow.)* I was just sitting home saying to myself, Rachel; you have *got* to get yourself a new phenakistoscope. The one you've got is just a mess. The radial slits are all shot. And when the radial slits are shot, there's just no hope. For a phenakistoscope. Or anything else, for that matter. *(She sits on the side of the bed, face in hands, near the point of crying for just a second, then pulls out of it and gets up.)* Oh dear, oh dear, oh dear, oh dear. Joe. Joe. Joe. Where did you go? *(Pause.)* All the way to.... *(Breaks off. Walks to dresser, sees dictionary.)* What have you been doing? Testing your sanity again, huh? What are you crazy or something? There's nothing wrong with you. *(Sees her reflection in the mirror. Pleased but critical.)* Five foot two. Five foot six, actually: Girls are bigger than ever. Lovely dark hair, fine hair. Opalescent skin. Lovely hips. Fine breasts. Nice legs. Nice, hell, great legs. Not bad ears; good hands. Slightly blah eyes, frankly; but then you can't have everything. *(Echo, breaking away. To herself.)* Can't have everything. What you are is probably a louse. A fool, of course, and a probable louse. Moral to a fault. And where you are a probable louse, Joe is a first-class, A-one definite louse without a doubt, and it is good to have a first-class definite louse out of your hair. *(She lights a cigarette.)* Four hundred and thirty-six dollars. *(Takes a puff; exhales.)* And thirty-eight cents. *(Wandering about.)* And several Government checks, like thirty, say. And about twenty odd forgeries, and about four cars, and four hundred and thirty-six dollars and thirty-eight cents.

AGNES. *(Offstage.)* I'm out. What are you up to?

RACHEL. *(Without paying attention. To herself.)* Oh, God. *(Sees herself in the mirror.)* Girl, you are a mess. Just a mess. *(Pause. Agnes enters. Without looking directly at Rachel, she goes to her bed, picking up the dictionary on her way and tossing it on her bed. Agnes has a cold. She is carrying a box of Kleenex, a section of the* Times *folded open to the cross-word, a pencil, a brush and comb, and anything else she can find. Her hair is wet, combed straight down. To herself.)* Well, what do you expect with last year's phenakistoscope?

AGNES. *(Without looking up, goes to her bed.)* Are you going to take a bath or what?

RACHEL. Take a bath? When did you start saying, "take a bath"? Take a bath, take a haircut, take a shower — I don't know what you're coming to.

AGNES. I got a cold.

RACHEL. What's that got to do with anything?

AGNES. Well, I abbreviate when I got a cold. *(She situates herself on the bed with the paraphernalia about her, including a dish of peanut brittle.)*

RACH L. *(Musing sadly.)* Four hundred and thirty-six dollars.

AGNES. *(Without looking up from the paper and brushing her hair.)* And thirty-eight cents.

RACHEL. I just wish I knew if I did the right thing.

AGNES. Look. A guy robs a store. If you turn him in, are you doing the right thing?

RACHEL. Do I know this guy or not?

AGNES. What guy?

RACHEL. Who robbed the store. In your hypothesis.

AGNES. Leave my hypothesis out of it. What difference does it make? He robbed a store — you turn him in.

RACHEL. He didn't rob a store.

AGNES. Are you going to take a bath or what?

RACHEL. I don't think so.

AGNES. You going to stay up and read all night or what?

RACHEL. Four hundred bucks. God.

AGNES. If you're going to start brooding I'm going to bed.

RACHEL. If just once we'd say to ourselves — you do that, girl, and you'll be sorry for it later.

AGNES. Yeah. Not bloody likely. *(Blowing her nose.)* Jesus, I'm coming down with something.

RACHEL. *(Studying her.)* You know what you are?

AGNES. Yeah? Make it good.

RACHEL. Susceptible.

AGNES. Susceptible. You hook the dud and I'm susceptible. I got a lousy job in lousy Kew Gardens and a lousy date tomorrow for lunch and a lousy dentist appointment and a lousy boss and a lousy love life and a roommate who takes out her aggressions on me. And all you can say is I'm susceptible. I'm dying. Face it, Agnes, you got a lousy life.

RACHEL. I meant susceptible to colds. Or drafts.

AGNES. "Agnes Mulligan: This Is Your Life!" And the TV screen goes blank for thirty minutes.

RACHEL. Why do you always have a cold? You've had a cold since I've known you.

AGNES. Maybe I'm allergic to you. I wear low-cut dresses is why. I knew when I was nine, with a name like Agnes, I was in for a dumpy figure and a big bust and low-cut dresses and susceptibility to drafts.

RACHEL. Well, don't wear them.

AGNES. *(Almost always speaks as if she is talking to herself.)* If I'da had any brains I'd have changed my name.

RACHEL. Why don t you?

AGNES. What's the point of having a big bust if you don't wear low-cut dresses. *(She puts the crossword on her lap, picks up the dictionary. Then, almost dreamily.)* What I can't wait for is a big house and about six handmaids and a big bed to sprawl all over. You know ... I want to keep my figure — what there is of it. After I'm married, I mean. I really do. I want to look as nice as possible. God, I think that's important.

RACHEL. Oh, would you shut up?

AGNES. *(Has opened the dictionary absently during the last speech. She shuts it and looks at Rachel.)* What the hell did you do to the dictionary?

RACHEL. Oh. I made a Rorschach.

AGNES. *(Pause.)* Yeah.

RACHEL. I was checking my responses. What does it look like to you?

AGNES. *(Reopening the dictionary, unamused.)* It looks like I better know the meaning and derivation of all the possible words between "obsecrate" and "ocelot."

RACHEL. What does it look like, though? Do you get an ostrich?

AGNES.   I don't get anything except mad. Jesus, Rachel.

RACHEL.   I'm sorry.

AGNES.   *(Pause.)* Good Lord. Nail polish, huh?

RACHEL.   Yeah. I thought maybe I was going insane.

AGNES.   And the simple act of pouring nail polish into the dictionary didn't confirm anything, huh?

RACHEL.   Don't pester me. Do I eat peanut brittle in bed? I thought you'd never get out of that tub. Don't you know not to leave a screwed-up girl alone with herself for three-quarters of an hour? *(She has said it comically, but suddenly feels sad, puts her head in her hands again.)*

AGNES.   Well, I was soaking. *(Notices her.)* Aw, come on, for Christ's sake.

RACHEL.   I only want to know if I did the right thing.

AGNES.   Look, a hundred of that was mine. He was a bum, what can I tell you? He was a bum and a thief and you turned him into the Secret Service and now what are you conjuring up? Lonely Joe in a cell? Well, forget it.

RACHEL.   You're not funny.

AGNES.   He was a bum. *(Aside.)* Damn, I'm all over peanut brittle.

RACHEL.   He was. Of course he was. But I had no idea he'd done any of that other.

AGNES.   How long had you known him?

RACHEL.   Three months.

AGNES.   Well in three months you're supposed to know everything about the guy? Every bank he's robbed, for Christ's sake?

RACHEL.   He hadn't robbed any banks.

AGNES.   Federal bank notes passed totaling into the thousands; you want to get technical, he's robbed a bank. A Federal bank at that. So you had fun; it wasn't worth it.

RACHEL.   You're a lot of help. I think I'm going over the edge and you sit there complacently sticking to the blanket.

AGNES.   *(Trying to wipe the blanket and Kleenex off her hands.)* This damn stuff. I'm growing fuzz. *(She sets the dish of candy on the table.)*

RACHEL.   What will they do to him, do you think?

AGNES.   *(Quickly, disgruntled.)* I think they'll hang him.

RACHEL.   *(Getting up.)* Stop it! Now you just stop it!

12

AGNES. Hey, come on. He'll go to jail. He stole my dough and your dough and the Federal Government's dough and God knows whose else's dough and he'll go to jail.

RACHEL. I just couldn't believe it.

AGNES. Yeah, me too.

RACHEL. We really had fun, too.

AGNES. Well, don't think about it, okay?

RACHEL. We really did.

AGNES. She says we really had fun, I tell her don't think about it, she says we really had fun. Jesus. Listen. You know what happened to the fag bookkeeper sits next to me out at work? He picked up this guy....

RACHEL. Agnes, I do not care what happened to the fag bookkeeper out at Standard Universal Plumbing.

AGNES. Standard Universal Fixtures. *(Pause. Firmly.)* There is no such thing as plumbing any more. *(Pause. Continuing.)* He took this guy he'd met up to —

RACHEL. Really! I don't —

AGNES. Look, do you think I'd trouble you if it wasn't pertinent? I'm not in the habit of telling you bedtime stories for the hell of it, am I? He picked up, good Lord, this guy! Apparently they just wander around till they see eye to eye with someone and then run right off the street and hit the sack, which, if you want to know my opinion, sounds a little capricious but not altogether impractical. Anyway, this big lug went home with him and "Stars Fell on Alabama," I suppose, or whatever the hell happens. Anyway, the next morning Henry waves good-by and two days later he sees this doll's picture in the paper — he'd been picked up for murder, my dear, of four or five fairies out in California and God knows how many more between here and there. Poor Henry almost died. He'd spent the night with this guy.

RACHEL. *(Pause.)* Fine! I'm sorry, I don't see the connection.

AGNES. You said you really had fun and you couldn't believe that Joe could possibly be —

RACHEL. — We happened to have been going together for three months! —

AGNES. — And you didn't know a damn thing about him —

RACHEL. You think a one night fling is the same —

13

AGNES. And you'd had some fun and you didn't know beans about him —

RACHEL. I didn't just pass him on the street!

AGNES. No, you didn't just meet him on a street —

RACHEL. Like your bookkeeper —

AGNES. You met him at Bickford's.

RACHEL. *(Defiantly.)* Longchamps! Honestly. I happen to be in love with him. That's why I'm wandering around this damn stupid — wondering — why the hell. Oh, Christ. *(She sits back on the bed, stretches out, rolls over on her stomach, sobs once.)*

AGNES. *(Getting up.)* Oh, come on. Have a box of Kleenex.

RACHEL. *(Her face buried in the pillow.)* I don't want them.

AGNES. They pop up.

RACHEL. Go away. Why did I say anything? What had it cost me really? Nothing. *(Agnes goes to the desk, gets a bottle of liquor out of the bottom drawer, fixes two drinks — just liquor, no mix.)*

AGNES. Honestly. Here. Have a shot. Me too, it's good for a cold. If I'm going to be running around nursing a roommate all night. Me? I'm always nursing someone else's broken heart. Just once I'd like a broken heart of my own.

RACHEL. *(Sitting up, takes the drink.)* You're great.

AGNES. I snore actually. Why don't you go to bed?

RACHEL. I can't. I don't think. You go on.... It isn't late, is it?

AGNES. No. I hate you like this, I pass up more good cracks.

RACHEL. I think maybe I should call in the morning.

AGNES. And tell them what? That he really didn't do it? Not here or in Denver or in Tucson? They knew twice what you did about him. *(Moving toward her purse on the vanity.)* I got a hangnail. Damn that typewriter.

RACHEL. I could drop the charges.

AGNES. *(Looking through her purse for a file.)* I doubt if they'd let him out for you. Besides, I don't know about you, but I'd be scared to death if he got out now.

RACHEL. I don't know what I should have done.

AGNES. Please don't worry about it. It's done. It's over; that's it.

RACHEL. *(Long sigh, not looking at Agnes.)* Yeah. *(Rachel is sitting gloomily, looking off into space.)*

AGNES. *(Finding something in her purse.)* You collect coins?

(Pause. No response.) I got a Tasmanian penny at Riker's yesterday.
RACHEL. *(Not listening.)* No.
AGNES. *(Temptingly.)* It's got some crazy fruit tree on it.
RACHEL. *(Not listening.)* No.
AGNES. *(Two fingers in the air, making a hand shadow.)* See the rabbit? *(Pause.)* You going to bed soon? Why don't you read something?
RACHEL. I tried it.
AGNES. Turn on the radio.
RACHEL. I tried it.
AGNES. What haven't you tried?
RACHEL. Oh, I'm being such a lunk. Really. Who's your lunch with?
AGNES. The boss's son. Tonsils. I told you about him. *(Nasally.)* He talks like that. And with a Harvard accent yet. He's got the kind of face, I swear as soon as it gets warm he's going to put on a funny pair of sunglasses. *(Pause.)* I feel I should sympathize with you, but honestly, Rachel, I've seen this happen I'll bet ten times since I've been living with you.
RACHEL. Not exactly this.
AGNES. And you say, "not exactly this" every time. It's a bore; you know what I mean?
RACHEL. All right. It's a bore. I couldn't agree more. How many boyfriends have I had? Since you've been here? Not so many.
AGNES. I'm not your datebook. I don't know.
RACHEL. Since you've known me?
AGNES. I don't know. What am I?
RACHEL. Roger. Just after you moved in.
AGNES. Floyd. You'd just broke up with.
RACHEL. Then Roger.
AGNES. Then Val.
RACHEL. Tom. Then Val.
AGNES. And Marvin. What a loser he was.
RACHEL. And Joe. Six. God. It's just too much.
AGNES. In what? Nine months. Not even a year.
RACHEL. They were nice guys, though. All of them, really.
AGNES. Oh, charmers. All. Burghers of Calais.

15

RACHEL.   It's too much.

AGNES.   It's an unearthly waste of time, you know? You know what you could do in nine months?

RACHEL.   Very funny.

AGNES.   I wasn't even *thinking* that! Jesus! I meant like get to know someone. Get married — get engaged, at least.

RACHEL.   Well, with Joe it was nearly three months. *(Looks aside at the phone, then reaches for it and sets it in her lap.)* Oh, God.

AGNES.   *(At the vanity dresser, still filing her nails, she is not looking at Rachel. She drops her file.)* Fuck! *(Bends to pick it up.)* I've got to quit saying that. Jesus. *(Looking at Rachel now, who is very slowly dialing a number.)* Rachel. *(No response. Firmly, flatly.)* Rachel.

RACHEL.   *(Not listening.)* What?

AGNES.   *(Firmly, flatly.)* If you're calling your mother I'm moving out.

RACHEL.   *(Not listening.)* What?

AGNES.   *(Same inflection.)* I said if you're calling your mother I'm moving out. Out into the street, into the rain. I don't care; I'll be happier there. I'll catch pneumonia, I'll go to Saint Vincent's Hospital, I'll be happier there, believe me.

RACHEL.   *(Putting the phone down.)* What's wrong?

AGNES.   Nothing's wrong, I've just had it with the Daisy Mae routine.

RACHEL.   It isn't that bad.

AGNES.   You are on that phone for one minute and you have an accent strong enough to paper the walls. And I've lived with one Southern girl and couldn't take that, but this nightly metamorphosis bit I don't need.

RACHEL.   Well, maybe it would help. There are times when you feel like calling your mother; what's wrong with that?

AGNES.   Well, then; call my mother. But you get a line from here to Dogpatch, Virginia, and I'm moving out. I can't take it. I don't intend to sit here and listen to it. The days of the Cotton Queen are over as far as I'm concerned.

RACHEL.   It isn't Dogpatch; I wish you'd quit saying that.

AGNES.   What is it?

RACHEL.   Cullerton.

AGNES.   *(Flatly.)* Cullerton. Virginia.

16

RACHEL. North Carolina.

AGNES. North Carolina. Jesus. How long did it take you to learn to lose the drawl?

RACHEL. How long? About five years.

AGNES. Five years. To learn not to drawl. *(To herself.)* Van Gogh didn't study that long to learn. Of course he couldn't drawl. *(Winces, turns to the mirror.)* I'm going to put up my hair. I wasn't going to, but if we're up for the night.

RACHEL. Go on to bed. I think I will.

AGNES. *(Looks into the mirror.)* Oh, Jesus. *(Looks away blankly. Count ten. Looks back blankly. Count ten.)* Agnes, you're a vision. *(To Rachel, without turning around. Rachel slides under the covers of her bed, opens a magazine, doesn't read it.)* You know, three years ago I had kinky hair.

RACHEL. *(Without listening.)* No kidding.

AGNES. I had it straightened. *(Pause.)* Ever since I've had straight hair.

RACHEL. Why don't you just let it be straight; it looks nice like that.

AGNES. No. What I'm not is Veronica Lake. I used to go to this beautician — this gal. Nearly killed me. Inside. She says, Agnes — she was Jewish, you know — Agnes, she says, I'll do wonders for you — you won't recognize yourself. Your own mother won't know you. For nearly a year, every week. She'd comb me out and reset me exactly the same. Agnes, I'll do wonders for you. I came out looking exactly the same as I went in. Solid year.

RACHEL. Why did you keep going back to her then? *(Agnes begins to set her hair, rolling it onto large rollers and slipping a bobby pin onto the roller. This is a comically realistic process, done quite matter-of-factly.)*

AGNES. I don't know. It's just nice to run into a positive attitude once in a while. I finally quit. She called me up after a couple of weeks, wanted to know what happened. I didn't have the heart to tell her my mother still recognized me. I told the beautician I'd bought a wig. *(Rachel laughs.)* She tells me — oh, Agnes — you gotta bring it over. I do wonders with wigs. Your own mother won't recognize.... *(Pause.)* You gonna stay up all night or what?

RACHEL. I don't know. *(She stretches out in bed.)*

AGNES.   Why did you ask for the bathroom if you don't want to shower or something, huh?

RACHEL.   Look — Agnes — *(Sitting up. Rather intense.)* Can we talk? Straight on this? So I can decide what I think for a minute, huh? Really, now — just straight for a minute or two and I'll be all right. I'll swear I don't know what the hell I'm going to do from here if I don't straighten myself out on this. I don't want to call Mom any more than you want me to, but I just want to —

AGNES.   *(Getting up, she goes for a cigarette.)* Sure. Of course we can; talk to Doctor Muller. My fees are reasonable.

RACHEL.   No, now — not even like that — just straight. So I know what I feel, or think or something! Sit down, now; stop flying around. See, I did like Joe and an awfully lot, too —

AGNES.   *(She has lit the cigarette. She sits down on the side of the bed opposite the table.)* Fine. Okay.

RACHEL.   Well, don't interrupt! God.

AGNES.   Okay, okay.

RACHEL.   While you wrinkled up in that damn tub I honestly thought I was losing my mind; you come back in here and I say, Agnes: I think I'm losing my mind, could you take a minute out of your life to listen to me and I get twenty minutes of Charlie Chaplin.

AGNES.   Okay! *(Pause.)* So go on.

RACHEL.   I'm sorry. It's just, Jesus. I don't know anything; I just can't seem to do something that doesn't backfire, boomerang in my face. Blow up right in my face. I do something heatedly, because I'm mad and it's the right thing to do, I know — and then the whole thing blows up in my face. They're practically ready to hang Joe and all because I turned him in for filching some money from us. Not that much, really, either; I didn't talk to him, I just turned him in. God knows what kind of fix he was in to take money from us. *(A rapid exchange follows between Agnes and Rachel.)*

AGNES.   You want a cigarette?

RACHEL.   I just ... NO! God! I don't want a cigarette.

AGNES.   Okay, so you don't want a cigarette.

RACHEL.   I just put one out. I have no urge for a cigarette at all. Thank you.

AGNES.   I only asked, don't make a production out of it!

18

RACHEL. Well, I do not want a cigarette.

AGNES. Okay.

RACHEL. Is there anything else?

AGNES. All right, I said. *Christ!*

RACHEL. *(Intensely.)* Well I'm trying to say something and little Miss Helpful Agnes butts in with —

AGNES. Would you hand me the ashtray anyway?

RACHEL. *(Takes the ashtray, slams it down on the bed beside Agnes. Very loud. Jerky.)* CHRIST! Here! Cram it.

AGNES. I merely asked for the ashtray. *(Rachel looks away, disgusted. Pause.)* Any particular place you'd like me to cram it? *(Silence.)* Well, I'm waiting for you to go on.

RACHEL. *(Still looking the other way. Quietly.)* Whenever you're ready.

AGNES. I'm ready.

RACHEL. *(Still not looking at Agnes.)* There's no point in my talking to myself. I could talk to myself by myself.

AGNES. I was listening to you.

RACHEL. *(Beginning to get tired, weary.)* Sure.

AGNES. I was. I heard every feeble-minded word you said.

RACHEL. Sure.

AGNES. You want me to repeat it?

RACHEL. No.

AGNES. You said, "God knows what kind of fix he was in to have to take money from us."

RACHEL. *(Silence. Then she turns to Agnes.)* Did I?

AGNES. You did. You said you do something and it blows up in your face; boomerangs, orangoutangs, backfires. And you do what's right and an innocent guy — which is a lie — is going to get hanged — which is a lie, and, "God knows what kind of fix he was in to have taken money from us." One more word and you'd have said, "It's only money."

RACHEL. Well, that's the stupidest thing I've ever said in my life then.

AGNES. *(Gets up.)* I'm going to roll my hair.

RACHEL. I can't even talk about him straight.

AGNES. What it boils down to is he was a damn good-looking stud and you —

19

RACHEL. Now, I resent that! For Christ's sake —

AGNES. Well, a good-looking guy then. And you're damn mad that you misjudged him and that you won't have him around again. And on top of that you trusted him enough to leave him here for a few hours when he was short — and you have to admit that he was very often short — and he took a month's pay from you. Now it's reasonable that you'd be pissed off. I would be too. I'd call the cops. *(She turns to the mirror and continues to roll her hair.)*

RACHEL. I did.

AGNES. Well, there you have it.

RACHEL. *(Sitting up in bed. Pause. Quietly; defensively.)* It isn't just physical.

AGNES. *(Not turning.)* When someone says it isn't just physical, you can be pretty sure it's just physical.

RACHEL *(Sliding back down into bed.)* I guess I am tired. I didn't sleep at all last night. Are you going to bed?

AGNES. Not now. I probably couldn't breathe anyway. I need a respirator.

RACHEL. How come?

AGNES. All night long I've been telling you I was a dying woman. I have a cold.

RACHEL. Oh.

AGNES. In my head.

RACHEL. *(Sleepily, from beneath the covers.)* Why don't you rub yourself with Vicks or something?

AGNES. Because I've got a luncheon date with the boss's son and I don't want to smell like Vicks. Even for him. I'll give him my cold first.

RACHEL. That s silly.

AGNES. *(Quite to herself.)* His soup would probably taste like menthol, for Christ's sake.

RACHEL. *(Flopping over on her other side.)* I think I'm going to sleep.

AGNES. *(Paying no attention.)* "Suddenly it's springtime." *(Drops one of the rollers.)* Fuck.... I've got to quit saying that. *(Looks at the roller; gets up and picks it up; goes back to the vanity.)* Get some sleep.

RACHEL. It won't look so bad tomorrow — I know. You know, though; you're probably right. I just miss him a lot and in a few days I'll see everything in a better perspective.

AGNES.   In a few days you'll be knocked up by some stud named Herkimer probably!

RACHEL.   *(Sitting up.)* I will not be knocked up by anybody.... In a few days or nothing.

AGNES.   Okay. I just meant, you've established a pattern by now. An orbit, so to speak, and by Thursday you'll be head-over-heels mad for someone totally different. You'll pass the sun again, so to speak.

RACHEL.   *(Under the covers again.)* I'm not that bad.

AGNES.   Very well, you're not that bad.

RACHEL.   At least my mother would have told me it would be better tomorrow. That's all I need to get to sleep probably.

AGNES.   *(Flatly.)* It'll be exactly the same tomorrow. "The world it was the old world yet. And I was I; my things were wet."

RACHEL.   *(Half sits up again, disgusted.) What?*

AGNES.   Nothing.

RACHEL.   What do you mean, "My things were wet?"

AGNES.   Nothing. It's a poem.

RACHEL.   I know it s a —

AGNES.   "Down in lovely muck I've lain; happy till I woke again. The world it was the old world yet and" —

RACHEL.   "And I was I, my things were wet." So all right. What's lovely about a muck?

AGNES.   He was drunk.

RACHEL.   At Ludlow fair or some place, I know he was drunk. What's lovely about a muck?

AGNES.   Well, maybe they pronounced it differently in Shropshire.

RACHEL.   Very funny. *(Flopping back down.)* Are you coming to bed? I'm dead. I've just knocked myself out.

AGNES.   Sure. You keep me awake all morning and ask me if I'm coming to bed.

RACHEL.   *(Covered by the blankets.)* I'm sorry.

AGNES.   Sure. You going to sleep or what?

RACHEL.   *(A little muffled.)* I said I was. If I can.

AGNES.   Well sleep it off. I don't know why you should worry any more about Joe than you did about whoever it was before. You've got to admit the pattern is evident there somewhere. Maybe you should really go to an analyst, you know? No joke. You probably have some kind of problem there somewhere. *(She turns to her. Rachel turns over. Agnes turns back to the mirror.)* I mean no one's normal. He's bound to find something. It might keep you away from dictionaries, you know? Jesus. *(Muffled noise from Rachel.)* Well, I say if it helps, do it. To hell with how funny it looks. God knows I'd like to find — I'm absolutely getting pneumonia. *(Gets up to get the box of Kleenex and carries it back to the vanity, talking all the while.)* I'm going to be a mess tomorrow. I probably won't make it to work, let alone lunch. A casual lunch, my God. I wonder what he'd think — stupid Charles — if he knew I was putting up my hair for him; catching pneumonia. No lie, I can't wait till summer to see what kind of sunglasses he's going to pop into the office with. *(Turns.)* Are you going to sleep? *(Pause. No reply.)* Well, crap. *(Turning back to mirror.)* I may be tendering my notice, anyway. You've gone through six men while I sit around and turn to fungus. It's just not a positive atmosphere for me, honey. Not quite. You're out with handsome Val or someone and I'm wondering if the boss's skinny, bony son will come up to the water cooler if I.... *(Trails of, becomes interested in the roller. Now to someone — as at dinner.)* No. No Stroganoff. No, I'm on a diet. *(Correcting herself.)* No. I will not admit that. Good or bad if he says Stroganoff and baked potatoes it's Stroganoff and baked potatoes. And sour cream. And beer. He's probably on a diet himself. He could fill out, God knows. *(Turning to Rachel.)* You know what Charles looks like? *(Pause.)* He looks like one of those little model men you make out of pipe cleaners when you're in grade school. *(Turning.)* Remember those? If I ever saw Charles without his clothes, he's so pale and white, I swear to God I'd laugh myself silly. He's Jewish, too. I'll bet his mother is a nervous wreck. I'll bet she thinks every woman on the block is pointing at her. Look, there goes Mrs. Schwartz; starving her children to death. Poor Charles. Shakes like a leaf. Of course Mrs. Schwartz wouldn't admit that either. No woman would admit her son was nervous; what's he got to be nervous about? The nerve of being nervous. My kid brother got an ulcer, my mother went to bed for three weeks, totally destroyed. Of course she spent about two thirds of her life totally destroyed. Upset — bawling. Weeks on end sometimes. My brother was great. He never paid the slightest attention to her; she'd get one of her spells and run off to bed bawling, it never bothered him for a minute. Off she'd go, the slightest provocation. Eric would say, "Mother's bedridden with the piss-offs again." I used to come home for a holiday or something and I'd say where's Mom and Eric would say, "Oh, she's bedridden with the piss-offs again." *(As if directly to someone, over lunch. Casually.)* You know, Charles, you've got nice eyes. You really have. Deep. I like brown eyes for a man. I don't like blue eyes, they always look weak or weepy. Either that or cold. You know? Brown eyes are warm; that's good. They're gentle. *(Quickly.)* Not weak, but gentle. *(Half to herself. Lightly.)* I used to want to have a girl; a little girl with blue eyes. For a girl that's good. So I used to always picture — God, idealize, really — very heavyset, blond men. Swiss types, you know. *(Back to Charles.)* But a son I'd want to have brown eyes. That's better for boys. *(Looks at the sleeve of her robe.)* You think? *(Almost embarrassed.)* I don't know anymore — Oh, yes; I got it at Saks. It was on sale, I believe. *(Breaking off, disgusted.)* Now, what the hell does he care where I got it? And it wasn't on sale, knucklehead. And it wasn't Saks. *(Concentrating on her hair.)* It was Bonds. Not that he'd know the damn difference. *(She drops a roller, it bounces across the floor. She picks up another without even looking after the first one.)* Fuck. *(Finishing her hair.)* I've got to quit saying that. *(This last said without listening to herself; second nature. She picks up a jar of cold cream, slowly, distantly, applies a dab to her lower lip. Pause. She sits still, staring off vacantly. A full thirty-second pause.)*

PROPERTY LIST

Dictionary (RACHEL)
Nail polish (RACHEL)
Cigarette (RACHEL, AGNES)
Lighter or matches (RACHEL, AGNES)
Kleenex (AGNES)
Section of the *Times* newspaper (AGNES)
Pencil (AGNES)
Brush (AGNES)
Comb (AGNES)
Dish of peanut brittle (AGNES)
Bottle of liquor (AGNES)
2 drinking glasses (AGNES)
Purse (AGNES) with:
    Tasmanian penny
    nail file
Magazine (RACHEL)
Box of large hair rollers (AGNES)
Bobby pins (AGNES)
Jar of cold cream (AGNES)

HOME FREE!

A Play in One Act

HOME FREE! was first presented by Joe Cino at the Caffe Cino, in New York City, on August 23, 1964. It was directed by, and the set and lighting designs were by, William Archibald; the cast was as follows:

LAWRENCE .... Michael Warren Powell
JOANNA .... Maya Kenin

HOME FREE! was produced by Theater 1965, as part of their New Playwrights Series, at the Cherry Lane Theatre, in New York City, on February 2, 1965. It was directed by Marshall W. Mason. The cast was as follows:

LAWRENCE .... Michael Warren Powell
JOANNA .... Joanna Miles

CHARACTERS

LAWRENCE BROWN
JOANNA BROWN
Both are dark, attractive, about twenty-five or twenty-six.

HOME FREE!

A small, cluttered room, where they eat and sleep. There may be a door to the kitchen, and there should be a front door. The room is several flights up. Important furnishings include a bed with a brightly colored quilt, a desk littered with paper, notebooks, etc. A candelabrum, a music box, perhaps a dresser for Joanna. There is a Ferris wheel which Lawrence has made; a large, colorful, highly decorated wheel which turns and has (perhaps ten or twelve) seats which swing as the wheel turns, all but two seats are on the wheel. A colorful box with a decorated lid, the Surprise Box, where gifts are placed. Perhaps a blackboard somewhere, and stools or chairs for Edna and Claypone, two imaginary characters who share the room. Joanna is about six months pregnant.

At rise we see Lawrence in the room alone. He is tapping the wall with the end of a coat hanger to get the attention of his "audience": Claypone and Edna, his students for the moment.

LAWRENCE.   Now, if you'll only pay attention! The Pleiades are called the Seven Sisters because they're grouped closely together and with the unaided eye you can only see seven of them. Actually they're about thirty stars in the whole cluster. Now you know that the universe is expanding; we discussed that — Billy, sit down and don't chew your eraser — we discussed that last time. I know your name isn't Billy, Claypone, but you're pre*tend*ing to be Billy: can't you just sit still like a good student? You're in Astronomy 101. If Edna can sit quietly, so can you. Now. As the universe is expanding and all of our galaxy is rotating, within the galaxy the stars are moving at incredible speeds in various directions. It's part of the expansion — Edna! — theory that all stars are moving farther and farther from each other. But the Seven Sisters, although they seem to be perfectly stationary to us, it has been proved that they are shooting away from the center — moving apart, at an incredible speed — every one getting farther from the others, so in a million years we won't be able to tell that they ever were a part of the same cluster. They're shooting out this way! *(Drawing, as with chalk, on the wall.)* And over here, and zoom — at about a hundred light-years a minute! Up and down and out and across — *(Getting uncontrollably excited, he starts tracing their path around the room as if following an exploded skyrocket.)* — and bang! And pow! And, if we was there, Whizz! Burn! Zing! Sssssstt Ssssssstt! Zooommmm! Kachowwie! Whamm! *(He has knocked some papers off the desk. He turns to Claypone, calming down.)* Hey, did I scare you? Did I? Where's Edna? *(His eyes focus under the desk across the room. Panting.)* You — come on back here, now. Come on. Sit down. You too, Claypone. It's part of the lesson. I'm busy now. You do something. I don't care; do anything. Don't bother me. *(He walks to the Ferris wheel, sitting, looking at it; turning it gently. To himself.)* No, no, if it went faster you wouldn't need the seats, because the gravity would throw you against the bars; either that or it would throw you off altogether. Well, that way is all right, too; it's just that it's a different ride altogether. You'll have to experiment and see which principle applies to this particular size model. Well it might mean the death of a hundred-thirty-seven human guinea pigs, but if it's for the advancement of entertainment, what's a sacrifice? I am an engineer, a scientist, I can only make the models; you can either use them or disregard my advancements. *(To Claypone and Edna.)* No, she went to the grocery — she'll be back in a minute. No, you can't go out and look for her. They'd grab you and lock you in jail in a minute. Because you don't watch for street lights. You do not — every time — *(He is getting nervous, frightened.)* — you go out, you get almost hit with some car or truck and it just drives me crazy trying to keep track of you. And besides you hate it out there. You know how you are! You make me so ashamed — stuttering! And not talking to a person and wilting into some corner like a shade plant. No. She'll be back! She went to the grocery to get a few things! *(Almost uncontrolled.)* And she said she'll be back and she will. You must stay here. No, you stay too. You're not going to leave me here alone; you'd wilt into some corner and they'd come and take you off. *(He forces himself down between the desk and bed, on the floor.)* She'll be right back. She promised. And we'll look in the Surprise Box. She promised. You promised. She just went out for a minute; and she'll be back like always and tell us about the adventure, now. *(Pause. Music. Sweetly now.)* You just sit now, like you were at a social tea with ice cream and cake and peppermint frosting and little sugar cookies with butter and almond flavoring. And little sugar crystals on top that are red and blue and yellow and white.... *(There is a soft but very urgent knock at the door.)* Shhhhhhh! *(Violently whispered to Claypone and Edna.)* Be quiet! *(The knock is repeated a little louder.)* Shhh!

JOANNA. *(From outside in a very urgent whisper.)* Quick, Lawrence. It's me. Quick; hurry. They're coming.

LAWRENCE. *(Hurries to the door, looks toward Claypone and Edna.)* It's okay, it's her. Sit down now and act like you've just been waiting nicely. Don't disappoint her. You just sit there. I'm coming.

JOANNA. *(From off.)* Hurry.

LAWRENCE. *(To Claypone and Edna.)* You be good. *(He unlocks the door. Joanna slips in and shuts it quickly. She stands just inside the door, her back to the wall. She locks the door quietly.)*

JOANNA. Shhh! She saw me! *(Still whispering.)* She saw me coming in. She was right behind me. She's right outside. Shhh!! Listen!

LAWRENCE. *(As soon as she comes in he begins to whine. Over above.)* Where have you been? They were just awful, they got so upset I hardly could control them.

JOANNA. Shhh! *(Now Lawrence listens at the door too.)*

LAWRENCE. *(Quickly to Claypone and Edna.)* Don't say anything.

JOANNA. She was right behind me. I think she's outside the door. Listen.

LAWRENCE. Did she see you?

JOANNA. I don't think so. *(Stops a moment; listens. In a normal voice, very casual.)* No, it's okay, now.

LAWRENCE. *(Still at the door.)* Shhh! Listen!

JOANNA. *(A little winded.)* No, it's okay now. Let me tell you!

LAWRENCE. I thought I heard something.

JOANNA. No, she's gone now. Sit down and I'll tell you about the adventure. *(Still not able to catch her breath, she lays her hand against her pregnant belly.)* Oh, poor old Tiberius and Coriolanus.

31

They must wonder what I'm doing running upstairs. I'm sorry, Tiberius. I'm sorry, Coriolanus. My heart is just beating away.

LAWRENCE. Shhh! You aren't listening.

JOANNA. No. It's okay now. My heart is just pounding like crazy.

LAWRENCE. *(Over, to Claypone and Edna.)* You two!

JOANNA. Am I turning blue?

LAWRENCE. *(Still whispering.)* That isn't fair!

JOANNA.. Feel how it's pounding. I shouldn't have run up those stairs but Pruneface was after me.

LAWRENCE. I'll feel the baby.

JOANNA. *(Disgusted.)* No. Claypone, sit down.

LAWRENCE. They were just awful while you were out. They were just terrible. I told Edna I was just gonna spank her good! If she didn't sit down and behave.

JOANNA. *(Taking off her head scarf.)* Well, she's young yet.

LAWRENCE. I said when my sister gets back here she's just gonna spank you good and proper.

JOANNA. Oh! *(Big announcement.)* He knows! Mr. Fishface knows. He asked about you. I've decided he knows the whole thing.

LAWRENCE. He asked after me?

JOANNA. Oh, he's getting so smarty, I'd like to just pinch him good. He said, "Where's your brother, Miss Brown?" And I said, "He isn't my brother, he's my husband; we're going to have a baby."

LAWRENCE. He said that?

JOANNA. Naturally I lied. He'll believe anything: I said, "He's my husband and he's in Bermuda just now and when he comes back he'll have a lovely dark tan." So you have to get a tan.

LAWRENCE. No.

JOANNA. Well, I'll think of something. Now. Sit down so I can tell you about the adventure.

LAWRENCE. Okay, Claypone sit there, she's going to tell us about the adventure. Edna, you stand there. And keep quiet!

JOANNA. Edna has to leave the room.

LAWRENCE. Edna, you must leave the room. Yes, you must! Through the kitchen and into the scullery and shut the door. And not a whimper out of you —

JOANNA. *(In exactly the same voice.)* — young miss! Go on this minute. *(She looks at Edna a moment.)* Well, I — !

LAWRENCE. What?

JOANNA. — No, I wouldn't have said that. You can't say things that I wouldn't have said when I was a little girl. *(She has started out reprovingly but softens now.)* You might grow up to be different than me. You must wear tall black stockings and a long gray skirt and a wine-colored apron and your hair will be combed straight back and pulled into a bun and clipped with — *(She makes a sudden, violent attack.)* Yes, it will, I did! *(Instantly sweet again.)* And clipped with a tortoise-shell bow. And you will sit with both your hands on your knees or folded in your lap and you will not think about what's between little boys' legs and you will speak when you're spoken to. *(She watches her go to the kitchen.)*

LAWRENCE. She's left.

JOANNA. She's listening. She has her ear against the door, she always does. *(Abruptly.)* Snoop! *(Listens.)* She's gone now. You know where she gets that — from that busybody landlady, Pruneface. *(She surveys Claypone and Lawrence and finds the situation satisfactory.)* Now. Actually, I only asked her to leave because I have an announcement to make. I will stand to — *(As she starts to rise she catches her heart — lightly. Her voice now is surprised, serious.)* Oh, golly! *(Sits.)*

LAWRENCE. *(Over a bit.)* No, no, no announcements. You have to tell us about the adventure.

JOANNA. No, wait, golly — I shouldn't run. Well. This is —

LAWRENCE. *(To Claypone.)* She's going to tell us about the adventure.

JOANNA. I will deliver my announcement from a seated position. Claypone, I want you to pay particular attention because you're involved.

LAWRENCE. I don't want to hear any old —

JOANNA. On my way outside to the grocery this afternoon, Miss Pruneface was in the hallway and she made me stop —

LAWRENCE. *(Over.)* What a silly thing to say — I don't know anybody by that name at all.

JOANNA. *(Without pause.)* And she said, "Mrs. Brown, I have told you before, you will have to move. You make too much noise as it is and" —

LAWRENCE. *(Over.)* She didn't say any such thing.

JOANNA. "And I'm afraid it will be impossible for you to live here after your baby is born."

LAWRENCE. *(Over a little.)* She did not. *(Both speak at once.)*

JOANNA. "And I'm afraid it will be impossible for you to live here with an infant. You know I told you that when you moved in here." And I told you — and I told her we would — I did — you were not either — I was there. I told her we would be out next week!

LAWRENCE. She didn't even say one word to you. She didn't say anything. I went out. I was there. I went out after you did and she said we could stay here like we have been and we could stay on, she said as long as we wanted to!

JOANNA. *(Wins.)* So there!

LAWRENCE. No.

JOANNA. She looks at me in the hall and shakes her finger at me.

LAWRENCE. You told her a hundred times that we were moving and she never says anything more. You say that every week.

JOANNA. No. She looks at me and she says I can't have the baby here — because they don't want the noise, Lawrence.

LAWRENCE. It doesn't matter what they want. *(There is a fast exchange between them.)*

JOANNA. They don't want the mess.

LAWRENCE. We just won't talk to her, then.

JOANNA. No, she'll throw us out in the street — !

LAWRENCE. We won't answer the door — Claypone, shut up!

JOANNA. *(Almost panicked.)* They're afraid of the baby, don't you know that?

LAWRENCE. — Claypone's making noise!

JOANNA. They don't want the pain!

LAWRENCE. We won't go! We're not going. If you're not going to tell me about the adventure, I'm going to call Edna back into the room — Claypone go get Edna.

JOANNA. You sit right back down.

LAWRENCE. Well, then, we're going to look in the Surprise Box — it's wonderful.

JOANNA. No. No, you can't until two o'clock today.

LAWRENCE. No, come on — it s especially lovely, I bet, today.

JOANNA. Not until after I tell you about the adventure. I have not told you.

LAWRENCE. Very well — first she's going to tell us about the adventure.

JOANNA. To begin — there was a shadow across the door downstairs.

LAWRENCE. The sun is shining.

JOANNA. *(She notices the interruption but goes on.)* It was all crooked because of the panels in the door, as usual; exactly the same number of squares in the sidewalk from here to the corner.

LAWRENCE. *(Quickly.)* Eighteen.

JOANNA. And — *(Pause. Sharply.)* I guess you just don't want to hear about it, do you?

LAWRENCE. *(Meaning "What did I do?")* What?

JOANNA. *(Continuing to look sharply at him.)* The same number of parking meters from here to the corner. *(Lawrence starts to speak up automatically; her look intensifies; he stops without really knowing why. When she is satisfied he is not going to interrupt she continues.)* Out of which eight were expired this morning. If you must know, I was thinking about the Ferris wheel most of the time I was out.

LAWRENCE. Do you want to look in the Surprise Box?

JOANNA. I don't think so; not till it's time. Unless you want to. It wasn't much of an adventure except for Mr. Fishface at the market. The Skinner was watching me so I couldn't slip anything. I think he's catching on. Old Fishface, though, he said: "Oh, how's your brother, Miss Brown?" I said, "It's Mrs. Brown, and he's not my brother as you are mistakenly referring to the gentleman whose company you've seen me in. That's Mr. Brown, and he's away in the Canary Islands trapping finches but we're expecting him shortly, Mr. Fishface. I'll give him your best."

LAWRENCE. Lie.

JOANNA. I said that. I did.

LAWRENCE. You didn't say, "Mr. Fishface."

JOANNA. I most certainly did.

LAWRENCE. Claypone, she didn't. *(They are beginning to laugh.)*

JOANNA. I did. And I said, "How's Mrs. Fishface?"

LAWRENCE. *(Laughing.)* You did not.

JOANNA. *(Laughing.)* And all the little tadpoles that must be swimming around at home. And all —

LAWRENCE. — And the pollywogs! And — *(They degenerate into a giggling mess, falling all over each other and slapping at each other. They fall onto the bed, giggling.)*

JOANNA. And the little baby perch.

LAWRENCE. And the whole Fishface family. *(They try to stop laughing. Joanna tries to sit up on the bed.)*

JOANNA. Come on. Be serious.

LAWRENCE. *(Pulling her back down.)* No.

JOANNA. *(Sitting up again.)* Yes — Go away, Claypone — sit down. *(To Lawrence.)* I don't know why we keep him around, he's so stupid. *(As he tries to pull her back down.)* Oh, don't — I get dizzy today. You know I can't play much at a time.

LAWRENCE. Oh, you're always dizzy. Now let's look in the Surprise Box.

JOANNA. No, wait! I forgot the most important part! A cat! *(This is used to draw his attention away from the Surprise Box as she slips a fountain pen into it a bit later.)* A yellow and gray and white and brown and —

LAWRENCE. Not brown. Lie!

JOANNA. Brown! With black ears — all spots — ran across from the market and under a parked car. I called to her but she wouldn't come. She only looked out from behind a tire and wouldn't come.

LAWRENCE. How did you know it was a she-cat?

JOANNA. Because she was fat and pregnant like me! No tomcat is going to have kittens.

LAWRENCE. Maybe you'll have kittens though! Spotted kittens!

JOANNA. Oh! Wouldn't that be *rare?* Why how rare! But I know I won't. I just couldn't. Nothing ever happens like that. Seldom ever.

LAWRENCE. Or pups! You never know what can happen. *(Joanna slips the pen into the box.)* Now let's look in the Surprise Box. *(The lid bumps softly.)* Did you peek? You peeked!

JOANNA. Lie! I never did. *(To Claypone.)* Tell him! Now see?

LAWRENCE. Okay. Let's look now. *(They walk to either side of the box.)*

JOANNA. Okay. *(They both close their eyes.)*

LAWRENCE.   Open it. *(She does.)*
JOANNA.   It's open. *(They open their eyes.)*
LAWRENCE.   A pen! Where did you find it?
JOANNA.   I have no idea where it came from. Maybe you can use it to write your book. *(Looking into the box with wonder.)* Ohh! I'll bet *someone* has sure been busy. Another seat for the Ferris wheel. *(She lifts it out gently.)* Oh, it's lovely. It's so lovely. This is the best one so far — it's so fragile!
LAWRENCE.   It's not too fragile, though, I don't think.
JOANNA.   Oh, no. It just looks —
LAWRENCE.   Where do you suppose it came from?
JOANNA.   I'll bet I know. I'll bet Lawrence Brown made it while I was out.
LAWRENCE.   Do you suppose....
JOANNA.   I certainly do suppose. Can I put it on? You can come over, Claypone, and watch.
LAWRENCE.   *(Nods.)* Carefully.
JOANNA.   Well, I won't break it. It's my surprise, after all. *(She sets it gently on the Ferris wheel.)* There. Is that all? Count them, Claypone.
LAWRENCE.   One more to go yet.
JOANNA.   Then it'll be totally finished.
LAWRENCE.   I'll bet no one has anything at all like this Ferris wheel.
JOANNA.   After you get just one more seat done —
LAWRENCE.   And then we can get in it and riiide like mad. *(Joanna is turning it very slowly.)* Easy! *(Said softly to Joanna, but as she starts to frown at him he adds quickly.)* Claypone, easy! *(Joanna automatically switches her frown to Claypone and they both frown briefly at him.)*
JOANNA.   Clutz. *(To Lawrence.)* Why we have to harbor a forty-three-year-old imbecile!
LAWRENCE.   *(As the Ferris wheel turns.)* Up we go.
JOANNA.   I don't think it's for us to ride. I think it's for the baby.
LAWRENCE.   Well, maybe all three — or you two and I'll turn.
JOANNA.   It's lovely. The last seat is the best, *I* think, anyway. Technically.
LAWRENCE   I can make this pen work. It's 14 carat gold.

JOANNA.   Where?

LAWRENCE.   There. And Parker. There.

JOANNA.   You can use it to write your book with.

LAWRENCE.   Hey, wonderful.

JOANNA.   What do you think we should call it, Lawrence?

LAWRENCE.   We? I get to name my book by my —

JOANNA.   No, no, no. Not your old book. You're so stupid.

LAWRENCE.   Lie!

JOANNA.   Claypone, isn't he stupid?

LAWRENCE.   Lie!

JOANNA.   Lie! Lawrence, you're stupid. My *baby*. What will we name it?

LAWRENCE.   *Our* baby.

JOANNA.   Our baby. What will we call it?

LAWRENCE.   I thought we settled on something yesterday. Boy or girl?

JOANNA.   I think girl.

LAWRENCE.   We'll name her — Miss Brown.

JOANNA.   *(Starting to say no.)* Well, why not? Perfect!

LAWRENCE.   The name will be perfect but I don't suppose we can expect the baby to be. I don't see how Miss Brown can help being deformed a little.

JOANNA.   Mmmm. Maybe no arms.

LAWRENCE.   Very well: no arms. At least she won't go around breaking things. You should concentrate on no voice box too.

JOANNA.   I don't think that's nice. You hate children. What kind of father is that? You have no business being a father at all if you hate children.

LAWRENCE.   I don't hate them. I hate the noise they make.

JOANNA.   Claypone, what can you do with a father who hates children?

LAWRENCE.   Well, what's so unusual about that? Besides, I don't hate them all. I think I begin to like them as soon as they're about fifteen years old.

JOANNA.   What do I do with her till then?

LAWRENCE.   I don't know. Send her to camp!

JOANNA.   *(Delighted at the idea.)* Of course. Send her to camp! Lackawalla Nursery, then Lackabellabella Camp and Miss Lackamannamanna's Home for Young Ladies.

LAWRENCE. And we'll be home riding the Ferris wheel. She's going to be no problem. *(Puts his head to Joanna's stomach.)* Are you going to be a problem, Miss Brown? What was that? You're all muffled. She says no.

JOANNA. Well, she's *diff*erent.

LAWRENCE. That's right, I'd forgotten.

JOANNA. *(Calling.)* You can come back now, Edna. Here, quick; kiss me. *(They kiss; she looks up as Edna enters.)* Oh, you weren't supposed to see that.

LAWRENCE. We were discussing things you're not old enough to understand, young lady. When you grow up maybe we'll tell you.

JOANNA. And maybe we won't.

LAWRENCE. Now let s go. I want to go off to bed. Come on.

JOANNA. No. Not now.

LAWRENCE. What kind of wife are you? It's part of the common law — you have to come when I tell you to.

JOANNA. I'm not your wife, I'm your sister.

LAWRENCE. Well, what kind of sister are you?

JOANNA. Only if I'm in agreement, and I don't fancy it. I want to at two o'clock. And nothing will —

LAWRENCE. Shhhh! Listen! I thought I heard something. That's twenty minutes. We can start now.

JOANNA. No, we won't start now. That isn't fair. There's no point in having a schedule if you don't stick to it religiously.

LAWRENCE. That's absurd.

JOANNA. Not at all. I have a very simple timetable here I've worked out. I'm quite mathematical, you know.

LAWRENCE. You are not mathematical at all. But I'll wait till two o'clock. And we can take Colonel Polarfuz with us. No, Edna, you slept with him last night. Wipe your nose!

JOANNA. Colonel Polarfuz was with us when I got pregnant. Every time you take the teddy bear I get pregnant.

LAWRENCE. That isn't true. He's been with us a hundred times and you haven't got pregnant but once.

JOANNA. Well, I will again. On top of Miss Brown. Or maybe Miss Brown will get pregnant. I'll have one and in three months I'll have another and the first thing you know I'll be turning them out like Volkswagens. Besides, when I have Miss Brown we have to move away.

LAWRENCE. No, Joanna. You can't have it if we have to move away.

JOANNA. Yes. Are we going to be good parents?

LAWRENCE. No.

JOANNA. Yes, we are.

LAWRENCE. Okay. The perfect parents. We can even get married.

JOANNA. But we have to move. The city isn't any place to prepare a child anyway. She can't grow up in the city —

LAWRENCE. — Ha! Prepare —

JOANNA. — What's funny? What's funny, Edna?

LAWRENCE. You said "prepare." *(To Edna.)* She said "prepare." The city is no place to prepare a child —

JOANNA. Well, it isn't.

LAWRENCE. *(Pretending to be a chef.)* To prepare one City Child, stew softly in mother's milk for two hours or until tender —

JOANNA. *(Joining in.)* — Turning frequently. City Children are poached in milk.

LAWRENCE. And in the country —

JOANNA. The Country Child is simmered in butter —

LAWRENCE. — And onions! *(Takes up a paper and pencil.)*

JOANNA. Chop twelve large red onions very fine —

LAWRENCE. That's too fast, let me write it down.

JOANNA. Chop twelve large Bermuda onions — we'll send it to *Good Housekeeping.* "Dear Cooking Editor. This recipe has been in our family for nine centuries" —

LAWRENCE. Generations. For nine generations.

JOANNA. — Grease lightly one Dutch oven.

LAWRENCE. And there has to be vegetables —

JOANNA. *(Quitting the game abruptly.)* We have to move anyway. Lady Pruneface looks at me every time I pass her in the hall or on the stairs. She looks at my bulging middle.

LAWRENCE. Well, if you'd learn to hold your stomach in like I told you.

JOANNA. She's thinking when Miss Brown comes out — we go out.

LAWRENCE. Maybe it won't be Miss Brown — maybe it'll be

kittens. With kittens she'd look the other way.

JOANNA.   I saw a cat!

LAWRENCE.   You told us. Honestly, sometimes you don't have all your marbles.

JOANNA.   I didn't tell you, Edna. Besides I saw another one: a dead one.

LAWRENCE.   Why didn't you get it? You should have brought it home free.

JOANNA.   It was too dead.

LAWRENCE.   What color?

JOANNA.   I couldn't tell.

LAWRENCE.   Gray then. Maybe it won't be kittens. Maybe it'll be pups. Pups she'd look the other way.

JOANNA.   Not a chance. It's too rare. It seldom ever happens anymore. You know that.

LAWRENCE.   It's almost two o'clock. I can't wait.

JOANNA.   You've got to. Sit down and wait. I don't mind going back on my word in front of Claypone, but not Edna. We should be an example to her. Why don't you work on your book?

LAWRENCE.   I decided to illustrate it myself.

JOANNA.   I didn't realize you were talented.

LAWRENCE.   I'm not, silly — but it's going to be very, very modern. *(To Edna.)* No, you can't! In color. *(He gets pencil and paper at his desk and sits.)* It'll be about Miss Brown and getting lost in the woods.

JOANNA.   And you must describe the woods in every possible detail. Every leaf and every bird.

LAWRENCE.   Very well. Don't bother me then, I'm going to write until two o'clock and then we'll go to bed. Now sit down. You too, Edna. And Claypone. Sit there. Now! And don't say a word. *(Pause while he thinks. Joanna sits.)*

JOANNA.   Don't chew your pencil.

LAWRENCE.   Shhhh!

JOANNA.   Well, I'm not sitting here watching you devour a perfectly good pencil. Chew a cigar or something if you want to chew.

LAWRENCE.   Shhhhh!

JOANNA.   *(Pause. Helpfully.)* Would you care for a stick of gum?

LAWRENCE. No thank you, Joanna. Just sit there and be still. *(Without looking up.)* Edna, stop fidgeting. *(Pause. He thinks and writes a few words. Joanna becomes restless. Gets up and wanders to the Surprise Box. She winds the music box, he reacts. She stops. Then opens music box for one note. He snorts. She closes it, turns around, and studies him.)*

JOANNA. A boy looked at me on the subway last night. *(Pause. No reaction.)* He said "hello"!

LAWRENCE. When? *(Pause. No reaction.)* When?

JOANNA. I didn't say anything, I looked the other way. Last night.

LAWRENCE. What'd he say?

JOANNA. He said hello and I turned my hand so he could see I was married and I looked the other way.

LAWRENCE. Lie. You went away with him.

JOANNA. Lie, I looked the other way. *(To Edna.)* I did too, young lady, you just shut your mouth or I'll wash it out with soap! *(To Lawrence.)* I looked the other way and he got off the train. Now go on writing.

LAWRENCE. What'd he look like?

JOANNA. I didn't notice.

LAWRENCE. What'd he look like?

JOANNA. I didn't notice, now go on writing. *(Beat.)* He had blond curly hair and a very square jaw and a sweater with a big red "R" on it. *(Quickly to Edna.)* I did not, young lady, you shut up!

LAWRENCE. Some college boy, they'll flirt with married women, it makes them feel big.

JOANNA. Well, I looked the other way and he got off the train. Aren't you going to write?

LAWRENCE. I can't do anything if you're going to talk all the time. You're just jealous because you don't have anything to do. I'll do something else.

JOANNA. Lie! I certainly am not.

LAWRENCE. Well, I'll do something else anyway. Let's go to bed.

JOANNA. Shhhh! *(Listens.)* Not now.

LAWRENCE. What? I'll move the clock up.

JOANNA. That isn't fair. You're a cheat.

LAWRENCE. You are. Edna, leave the room!

JOANNA. I said I wouldn't. *(To Edna.)* You sit right back down, young miss. You just do what I do. *(To Lawrence.)* Edna and Claypone can read. *(To them.)* You can read. I don't care — anything. *(To Lawrence.)* And you and I will talk about moving.

LAWRENCE. I won't talk about any such thing!

JOANNA. We have to talk about it. We have to. She's right behind the door and besides Miss Brown will probably be blue!

LAWRENCE. Not blue. Shut up about blue.

JOANNA. If I was a blue baby she'll be a blue baby. It's simple heredity.

LAWRENCE. You were not a blue baby. You just make it up so you'll sound exceptional.

JOANNA. Mother said I was a blue baby and they sewed me back up and I am too exceptional.

LAWRENCE. What does she know about it?.

JOANNA. ... Besides I can feel the catgut.

LAWRENCE. I don't want to hear about your pains and catgut. Honestly, sometimes you can really be nauseating.... *(Mumbling.)* Catgut.

JOANNA. I had another one.

LAWRENCE. I don't want to hear about it.

JOANNA. *(Holding her shoulder.)* I felt it here. Feel.

LAWRENCE. That shows what you know about it. Heart pains are felt in the bottom of the stomach.

JOANNA. Well, mine hurts me here. You know it does. You were scared once.

LAWRENCE. When was I? I was not. You were faking and I knew it.

JOANNA. Lawrence Brown, you were so.

LAWRENCE. Joanna Brown, I was not. I wasn't. You made it up; you did.

JOANNA. I didn't.

LAWRENCE. I wasn't. You never had one of your pains!

JOANNA. I feel it all the time.

LAWRENCE. I won't listen to you. I have to write.

JOANNA. *(Louder.)* I feel it in my shoulder like someone pinching me!

LAWRENCE. *(Louder.)* I won't listen to you. I'll sing!

JOANNA. *(Louder.)* I DO! I can feel it right now!

LAWRENCE. *(Singing loudly.)* My country tis of thee — sweet land of liberty! Of thee I sing! Land where! —

JOANNA. Okay! They are trying to read. You can at least be civil. I know it's difficult for you, but if you will only try.

LAWRENCE. You started it by faking.

JOANNA. Well, I feel it!

LAWRENCE. *(Sings two notes very loudly.)* Land where! —

JOANNA. But I won't talk about it. Shhh! Listen.

LAWRENCE. What?

JOANNA. Shhh! She's gone. You won't learn, will you?

LAWRENCE. Well, you started it by faking ... you think you're so very exceptional.

JOANNA. Well, I *am exceptional!*

LAWRENCE. You are not! You're blue and that's not exceptional.

JOANNA. You shut up!

LAWRENCE. Turn blue for me. Just once!

JOANNA. I. Will. Not!

LAWRENCE. You can t.

JOANNA. I could if I wanted to. I wouldn't be inclined to for you.

LAWRENCE. *(Pause.)* Are we really going to be turned out? Did she honestly say no children?

JOANNA. She only told us a dozen times.

LAWRENCE. Well, what does she expect a young married couple to do?

JOANNA. We're not married.

LAWRENCE. Well we told her we were. We'll get a lawyer.

JOANNA. We can't. He'd guess. You know how lawyers are. They'd even take away Miss Brown. *(To Edna.)* They can *have* you!

LAWRENCE. He'd guess from your eyes.

JOANNA. Certainly not! You'd tell him. You'd stammer and stutter and he'd know. You always stutter when you talk to anyone but me!

LAWRENCE. I do not!

JOANNA. You stutter and stammer and just wilt into a corner like some shade plant.

LAWRENCE. Stop.

JOANNA. You just can't — *(Whining.)* — cross the street — Oh,

I can't *talk* to anyone. Oh, that truck is going to hit me!

LAWRENCE. Don't.

JOANNA. *(Calmer.)* You always embarrass me when you talk to the landlady.

LAWRENCE. Well, I can't talk to Pruneface. She's wrinkled. She has white hair, that's the reason. *(Joanna smiles and doesn't speak.)* It is, too!

JOANNA. I didn't say a word. I agree with you. I really do. *(Pause.)* Mr. Fishface doesn't have white hair and you stutter to him!

LAWRENCE. He's got a fish —

JOANNA. I didn't hear you.

LAWRENCE. He s got —

JOANNA. I didn't say a word.

LAWRENCE. I have to write. Why don't we go to bed and play?

JOANNA. I'm not in the mood. You'd stutter.

LAWRENCE. Lie! That *was* a lie! Tell her, Claypone.

JOANNA. You're just a mess.

LAWRENCE. You are! You live in common law!

JOANNA. So do you.

LAWRENCE. So do you!

JOANNA. It's different with me. I'm a girl. *(To Edna.)* We girls are very exceptional.

LAWRENCE. You live in common law.

JOANNA. I was a blue baby! And besides, I have a pain.

LAWRENCE. I'll give you a pain. You always have a pain when you're in the wrong. I'll kiss it and make it well.

JOANNA. Go away. It feels like pinching. Really.

LAWRENCE. You're faking. You want attention because you're pregnant.

JOANNA. That's a perfectly acceptable reason. Ask any woman — until the child is born any woman is a very very special and wonderous thing. *(Regally.)* As a matter of fact, I'm royalty. I'm a queen! *(Simply.)* I have blue blood.

LAWRENCE. A queen! *(Music for two or three bars, very faint.)* A queen! I should have recognized it. Queens are always pregnant with somebody or other. Prince Claypone! Fetch her the crown. Lady Edna, Lady Edna — into the kitchen and supervise those wenches. Into the kitchen with you!

JOANNA. *(Assuming the air of a gruff queen.)* Bring me a pickled flamingo, Lady Edna!

LAWRENCE. *(Bringing a chair.)* Sit here on this throne. Up with your feet on the ottoman.

JOANNA. *(Kicking aside the chair.)* Down with the Ottomans! Behead every one of them. Barbarians! I won't have them in the kingdom! Where's my filet of flamingo? Behead that girl!

LAWRENCE. *(With a quilt from the bed.)* You must have a mantle. This robe, your pregnancy, was made by four hundred Hungarian virgins who went blind sewing seed pearls. *(Getting a candelabrum.)* And a scepter! Is there anything else, your pregnancy? *(He tucks in the quilt.)*

JOANNA. *(Gruffly.)* Careful with me, you fool. I'm with child! You're jostling the future king!

LAWRENCE. *(Excited. Again singing. Loud.)* For unto us a child is given. For unto us a son is born. And the government shall be upon his shoulders! And his name shall be —

JOANNA. Silence! Silence that racket or off with your shoulders!

LAWRENCE. Oh, no. Not that. Not that, your pregnancy. Not my shoulders! Throw me in the briar patch, but not my shoulders!

JOANNA. *(Saintly.)* I knight. Thee. *(Pause.)* Sir Stutter! Ha!

LAWRENCE. That's not fair! You're a whore. *(Takes away quilt.)* You're not a queen. Fetch your own filet of flamingos. Edna — forget the flamingos. She's not a queen, she's a whore.

JOANNA. Oh! I *am not!*

LAWRENCE. I bet you are!

JOANNA. I bet I am not!

LAWRENCE. I bet you go around trying to stir up some look in boys' eyes.

JOANNA. I bet I do not.

LAWRENCE. Lie!

JOANNA. Lie! I do not. Only you. You know it's true. I couldn't get away if I wanted to. Besides, now I'm pregnant.

LAWRENCE. I'd hold you in. *(Moving behind her.)* I'd bite the nape of your neck and pull you back like a tomcat.

JOANNA. *(Playfully.)* Ouch! It tickles.

LAWRENCE. Of course it tickles. Let's take a shower.

JOANNA.   No. Oh, sometimes you're really vulgar. Sometimes you really shock us.

LAWRENCE.   Shock you. I do not.

JOANNA.   You do, too. You do.

LAWRENCE.   Let me feel the baby. *(Reaches around her. To Edna.)* Do you want to feel the baby?

JOANNA.   *(To Edna.)* No! No, you can't. You'd hit. I know you.

LAWRENCE.   I think she's asleep. *(Joanna touches her shoulder.)*

JOANNA.   Ouch, Lawrence!

LAWRENCE.   I'm not hurting. You don't suppose she's asleep. Hey, wake up, Miss Brown. God, you don't suppose she's going to be lazy, do you? Edna, you knock over that Ferris wheel and I'll hit you good!

JOANNA.   Of course she's not going to be lazy.

LAWRENCE.   If there's anything I can't tolerate it's laziness. Why doesn't she kick or something?

JOANNA.   I like it when she takes these little cat naps —

LAWRENCE.   Do you suppose she'll really be a whole litter of kittens?

JOANNA.   Lord knows she kicks me enough when she's awake. *(To Edna.)* She's going to take after you, you little sadist. *(Touches her shoulder.)* Oh, golly.

LAWRENCE.   What s wrong?

JOANNA.   I had a little pain is all.

LAWRENCE.   Miss Brown kicked you!

JOANNA.   In the shoulder. You don't seem to realize that Mrs. Pruneface is just outside that door and she's going to kick us out onto the street and I have a pain.

LAWRENCE.   Oh, that! *(To Edna.)* Don't believe her.

JOANNA.   You never believe anything I say. None of you. Well, you'll see.

LAWRENCE.   Hey. Come to bed with me now.

JOANNA.   I will, I guess. If you'll only be quiet. It's nearly time.

LAWRENCE.   *(Singing.)* It's nearly time, it's nearly time.

JOANNA.   And if you'll promise to talk about moving away afterwards.

LAWRENCE.   Afterwards they lay on the soft grass and talked about moving away.

JOANNA. *(Happy.)* I wish I wasn't pinching.

LAWRENCE. I'll teach you to pinch.

JOANNA. The whole world pinches me!

LAWRENCE. *(Singing.)* He's got the whole world — between his finger and thumb.

JOANNA. You always sing when I say we'll go to bed!

LAWRENCE. It makes me happy. I like it.

JOANNA. That's all you know. Hop in bed. You're a funny rabbit.

LAWRENCE. I'm a funny rabbit. *(To Edna.)* Are you a funny rabbit?

JOANNA. Impossible rabbit. I love an impossible rabbit. Oh, God!

LAWRENCE. What?

JOANNA. Well, think of all the number of offspring rabbits have.

LAWRENCE. Wonderful.

JOANNA. That's all perfectly well for the buck — but I have to bear all those scratchy little monsters. Fuzzy little monsters.

LAWRENCE. You'll die laughing! It sounds like fun.

JOANNA. Everything sounds like fun to you.

LAWRENCE. Everything is.

JOANNA. How do you suppose a female rabbit keeps from giggling? I mean, think how furry a baby rabbit is.

LAWRENCE. They really are, you know. *(To Edna.)* Of course they are, Edna. And long tickly ears. But giggling isn't bad.

JOANNA. Well, maybe not — but it certainly would destroy the seriousness of the situation.

LAWRENCE. You giggle better than any rabbit anyway.

JOANNA. Oh, I never giggle. *(Picks up music box.)*

LAWRENCE. Oh, you don't?

JOANNA. What?

LAWRENCE. You never giggle. You don't, huh? *(He starts advancing slowly toward her.)*

JOANNA. No-o-o-a.

LAWRENCE. You don't giggle ever, huh?

JOANNA. Now you stay away. I can't play like that. *(She is smiling.)*

LAWRENCE. Not even with someone playing the piano on your ribs? Get back, Claypone.

JOANNA. *(Touching her shoulder.)* You stay away now. I don't giggle. *(They are laughing now.)*
LAWRENCE. Edna? Did you hear what she said? She said she doesn't snicker. Not even a little. Whatta you think of that?
JOANNA. Now that isn't true. *(They are circling the room.)* I didn't say I don't snicker. I said I don't giggle. I snicker all the time.
LAWRENCE. You giggle too. Admit it.
JOANNA. I snicker like a horse. It's *disgusting* the way I snicker. *(She half throws, half lays the music box on a chair.)* Move back, now. Edna, don't you help him. *(There is a full-scale chase.)*
LAWRENCE. You re going to giggle. *(He knocks the chair over.)*
JOANNA. Stay back, I said! *(From the floor the music box plays.)*
LAWRENCE. No. We're going to make you giggle.
JOANNA. No, you aren't.
LAWRENCE. I am. Claypone, head her off.
JOANNA. Don't do it, Claypone. I'll tell Mother on you.
LAWRENCE. Mother's in heaven and Mother can't hear you.
JOANNA. Mother's in Hoboken and if I yell loud enough she'll *hear me.* The whole *building* will hear me!
LAWRENCE. They'll hear you giggle when I catch you.
JOANNA. They won't! *(She pulls out a chair and runs behind the table. Sudden stop. Scream. Joanna's expression is one of terror and great pain. Lawrence is still playing. He thinks she is joking.)*
LAWRENCE. Everyone will hear you laugh your —
JOANNA. Get away. *(She can't speak further.)*
LAWRENCE. What's wrong? *(She turns to him.)* Oh, come on! That's not fair. That isn't fair. Edna, don't believe her, she's joking. She's pretending.
JOANNA. *(Starting to collapse.)* It's pinching me....
LAWRENCE. I don't believe you. *(Still he takes her and starts to help her to the bed.)*
JOANNA. Oh, really, Lawrence, really!
LAWRENCE. I don't believe you. That's foolishness. I'm not going to get frightened again, if that's what you're trying.
JOANNA. Am I blue?
LAWRENCE. Really? You truly hurt? *(He is getting scared and excited.)* I'll help you, don't worry. I'll get you something. What do you want, Joanna?

49

JOANNA. A doctor. Oh, please.

LAWRENCE. A doctor? They know everything. I'll get you a doctor. *(But he stays by the bed.)* I will.

JOANNA. Lawrence, go. Go on, hurry.

LAWRENCE. I will. I'll get you anything, Joanna. *(Panicked.)* Tell me what you want, rabbit.

JOANNA. Downstairs and on the corner — get me a doctor.

LAWRENCE. No, now I can't go out there, Joanna, you know I don't go out there, you said I —

JOANNA. Please, Lawrence —

LAWRENCE. — *never had* to go out there — now, I can't do something —

JOANNA. *(Screams, but the wind cuts away from her voice.)* No. Go on, Lawrence. Look, it's okay. It's okay. There's nothing out there that will hurt you, it's — *(Lawrence has gone to the door.)*

LAWRENCE. No, she's out there — she's right on the other side of the door. I can't go out there.

JOANNA. Lawrence, it's never been like this. Go on!

LAWRENCE. *(Crumpling at the door.)* No, I can't. I can't. Don't make me. Don't make me. Please don't make me. I can't go out — They'll take me off — I can't go, don't make me, Joanna, please don't.

JOANNA. *(Over the above, coaxingly.)* Lawrence, look, baby, it's okay, baby, there's nobody out there who can hurt you, baby, Lawrence, for me. Please. Please. *(Her strength fails.)*

LAWRENCE. Joanna? Say things to me, Joanna. *(She looks at him.)* Joanna?

JOANNA. Please. *(She takes a jar and knocks it violently against the wall, calling.)* Miss Williams! Miss Williams!

LAWRENCE. *NO!* Don't call old Pruneface! I'll get you a doctor, I really will, Joanna. It's okay. Quick, quick, EDNA! Put on your coat, child, this is an emergency. *(He runs and opens the door just enough for Edna to squeeze through.)* As fast as you can or she'll die. There's a doctor's sign over the drugstore on the corner.

JOANNA. No, Lawrence! You go. You go. YOU GO!

LAWRENCE. *(Turning to her.)* It's all right. She went for him. You have to be patient. Can I get you something? You'd feel better if you sat up and talked, I'll bet. *(She has tried to sit up. She falls back.)*

Here, I'll sit by you and hold your hand. *(He takes her hand; it falls lifeless and unnoticed from his.)* Now, don't go to sleep, she'll be right back in no time. I told her to hurry. It's after two o'clock already. I wish you'd sit up and — I know what — I want to show you something. *(He gets a seat for the Ferris wheel from the table where he'd hidden it.)* If there's something in the Surprise Box. *(He puts it in but is too excited to leave it there.)* Joanna, I bet there's something in the Surprise Box. *(He opens it.)* I wonder.... Look. *(He brings it over to her.)* See? I made two of them and this one is.... If I put it on the Ferris wheel, will you sit up? If — I tell you — you can put the last one on.... If I — what if I — look. *(He sets it on the wheel.)* Joanna? Look at that! It's all finished, Joanna. Are you going to sleep? It's all finished — you're supposed to be the very first one to turn it.... Look, if I let you.... If I turned it for you then you — would you — then would you? Huh? Look, what ... if I see? *(He turns it slowly around.)* See? Well, If I If I If I If I took — If I went — let you take — if I got, then, would.... If I then would ... you ... would ... you....

PROPERTY LIST

Coat hanger (LAURENCE)
Papers (LAURENCE)
Ferris wheel (LAURENCE)
Ferris wheel seats (JOANNA, LAURENCE)
Fountain pen (JOANNA)
Surprise box (JOANNA)
Paper (LAURENCE)
Pencil (LAURENCE)
Music box (JOANNA)
Quilt (LAURENCE)
Jar (JOANNA)